Unwind

CreativeColoringBooksForAdults.com

MandaLove Press

www.CreativeColoringBooksForAdults.com

www.Facebook.com/CreativeColoringBooks

Published by MandaLove Press, LLC

First Edition Printed September 2015

ISBN-13:978-0692540985

ISB-10:0692540989

Printed in the United States of America

Distributed by Adult Coloring Book Creative

Hours of fun and relaxation inside ...

Relax, have fun, and give your inner artist free reign with our brand new coloring book, **Unwind**.

Within the pages of **Unwind** you'll find 30 original, one-of-a-kind mandala and repeating pattern designs. **Unwind** is filled with hours of creative fun for the kids or relaxing, quiet time for you. Leave behind the stress of the day and spend some time coloring! It's not only fun, it's good for you!

The mandala designs and repeating pattern pages in **Unwind** are printed one to a page, but markers can bleed through even the best paper. Two blotter pages have been added to the back of the book for you to use to keep your artwork pristine.

Free coloring pages ...

Subscribe to our newsletter today and we'll send you a free set of bonus mandalas to color. You'll also have a chance to win a brand new coloring book!

We choose a new winner every month:
http://CreativeColoringBooksForAdults.SubscribeMeNow.com/

Join us on Facebook and you'll have access to free coloring pages and more chances to win free coloring supplies and coloring books:
https://www.Facebook.com/CreativeColoringBooks

Look for our coloring books on Amazon and at your local bookstore!

Thank you for supporting independent artists!

Notes

Notes

Blotter Page

Two blotter pages have been included for your convenience. Remove one or both and use them as a barrier between the page you are coloring and the next.

The designs in this book have been printed on one side of the page, but markers often bleed through even the best paper. To keep your art work pristine as you color and create, use another piece of paper as a buffer between the pages of this book, or use a thin piece of cardboard (cut one side from a cereal box, or use the thin cardboard insert that is found inside a new shirt)

Blotter Page

Two blotter pages have been included for your convenience. Remove one or both and use them as a barrier between the page you are coloring and the next.

The designs in this book have been printed on one side of the page, but markers often bleed through even the best paper. To keep your art work pristine as you color and create, use another piece of paper as a buffer between the pages of this book, or use a thin piece of cardboard (cut one side from a cereal box, or use the thin cardboard insert that is found inside a new shirt)

Thank you for buying a MandaLove Coloring Book!

♥

We've put together a FREE Bonus package of new mandalas, available for you to download at this link:

CreativeColoringBooksForAdults.SubscribeMeNow.com

♥

Join us on Facebook and take part in coloring contests and free book and supply give-aways. Show us your completed designs!

Facebook.com/CreativeColoringBooks

♥

Look for our coloring books on Amazon and at your local bookstore!

www.Amazon.com/author/CreativeColoringBooks

♥

www.ingramcontent.com/pod-product-compliance
Lightning Source LLC
Chambersburg PA
CBHW081222020426
42331CB00012B/3073